For my parents, who have always loved, supported and nurtured the independent spirit within me.

Alligator

Try learning something new.

Butterfly

Embrace change.

Cat

Listen to your intuition.

Dog

Be playful.

Elephant

Take care of yourself.

Frog

Trust yourself.

Goat

Believe in yourself.

Hedgehog

Be joyful.

Insects

Share with a friend.

Jellyfish

Be yourself!

Kangaroo

Be thankful.

Llama

Love yourself!

Monkey

Have fun!

Nightingale

Have some quiet time.

Ostrich

Clean something!

Pig

Be confident!

Quail

Spend time with your family.

Rooster

Listen to your heart.

Snail

Relax and enjoy the day.

Tiger

You are strong!

Unicorn

Use your imagination!

Vixen Fox

Get creative!

Whale

Listen to your senses.

X-Ray Tetra Fish

Listen to your emotions.

Yak

Show love to your family and friends.

Zebra

Be yourself!

Pay attention to the animals around you, they might have a message for you!

www.ingramcontent.com/pod-product-compliance
Lightning Source LLC
Chambersburg PA
CBHW051526220426
43209CB00106B/1681